ADAM LISTENS TO HIS MOM

Dalia Ramzi Mohammad

Editor: Noor Hammoud
Copyright ©2019 by Dalia Ramzi Mohammad

"Adaaam!" his mom called,
"Clean your room!"
Adam did not feel like cleaning.
He was lying on the couch watching television.
"Adam, come upstairs!" his mom pleaded.
"I don't want to!" he replied.
His mom was upset.

Later that day,
Adam was drawing when his sister Sara asked,
"Can I please use that pencil?"
Adam frowned and snatched it away.
"No way!" he snapped.
His mom said,
"Adam, share with your sister."
"No!" Adam insisted.

That evening during dinner,
Adam played with his food.
"Adam," his mom said, "eat your meal."
"I don't want to!"
Adam whined and pushed his plate away.
His mom's face looked sad.

Adam went upstairs.
His room was still messy
and his tummy was grumbling.
He was upset.
As he was getting ready for bed,
he thought about his mom's face.
He did not want her to be sad.
He loved her so much.
Then Adam remembered how Allah
tells us to listen to our parents.

The next morning,

Adam made his bed and cleaned his room.

His mom walked in and was surprised.

She exclaimed, "Wow Adam!"

He gave his mom a hug.

"I'm sorry I didn't listen to you before," he said.

"It's okay, we learn and grow from our mistakes,"

his Mom replied.

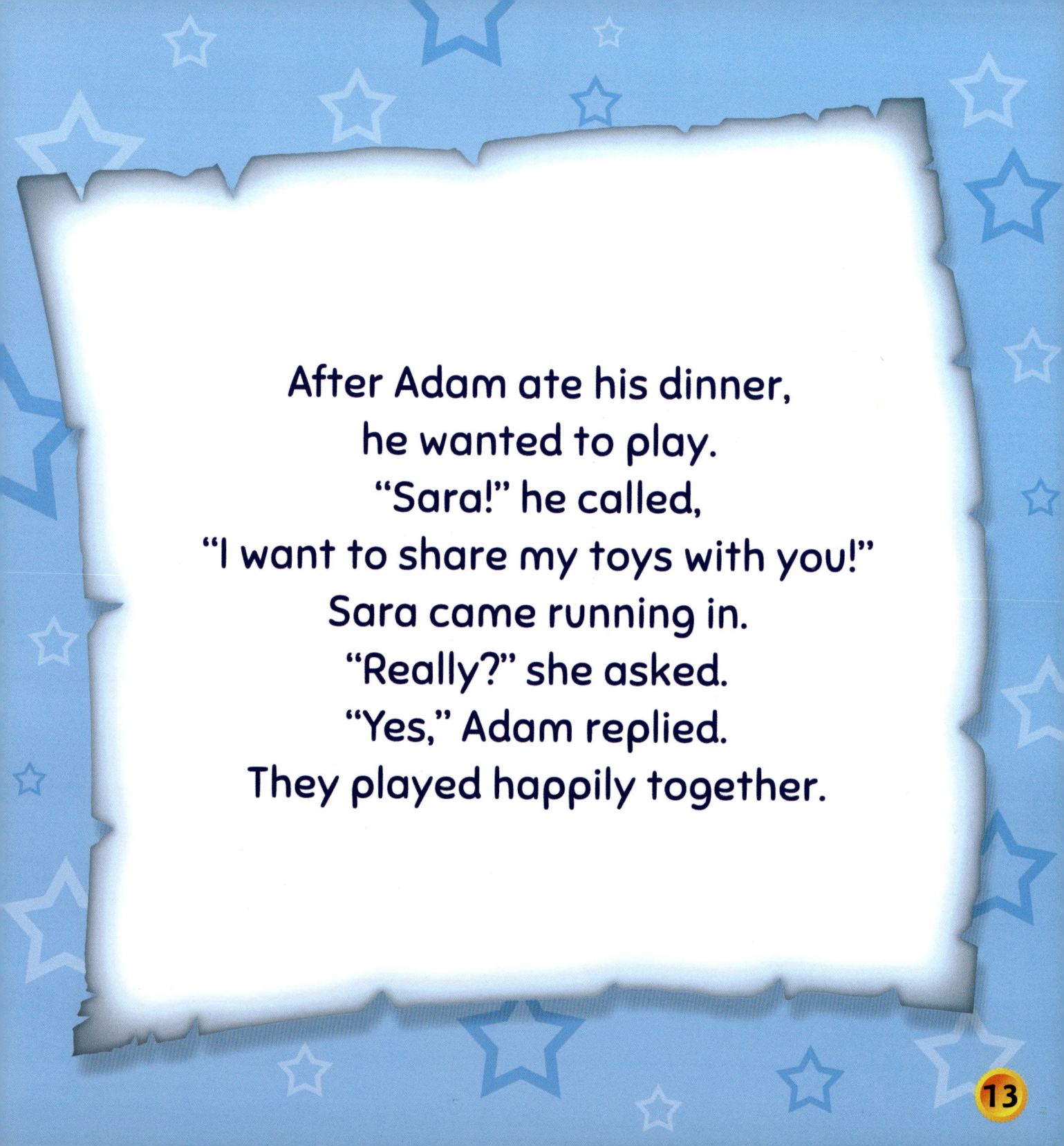

After Adam ate his dinner,
he wanted to play.
"Sara!" he called,
"I want to share my toys with you!"
Sara came running in.
"Really?" she asked.
"Yes," Adam replied.
They played happily together.

Adam felt good.
His room was clean,
his tummy was full,
and he had fun with his sister.
That night as he laid his head on his pillow,
he realized that everything his mom told him
to do was because it was good for him.
From that day on,
Adam tried his best to listen to his mom,
which made them both very happy.

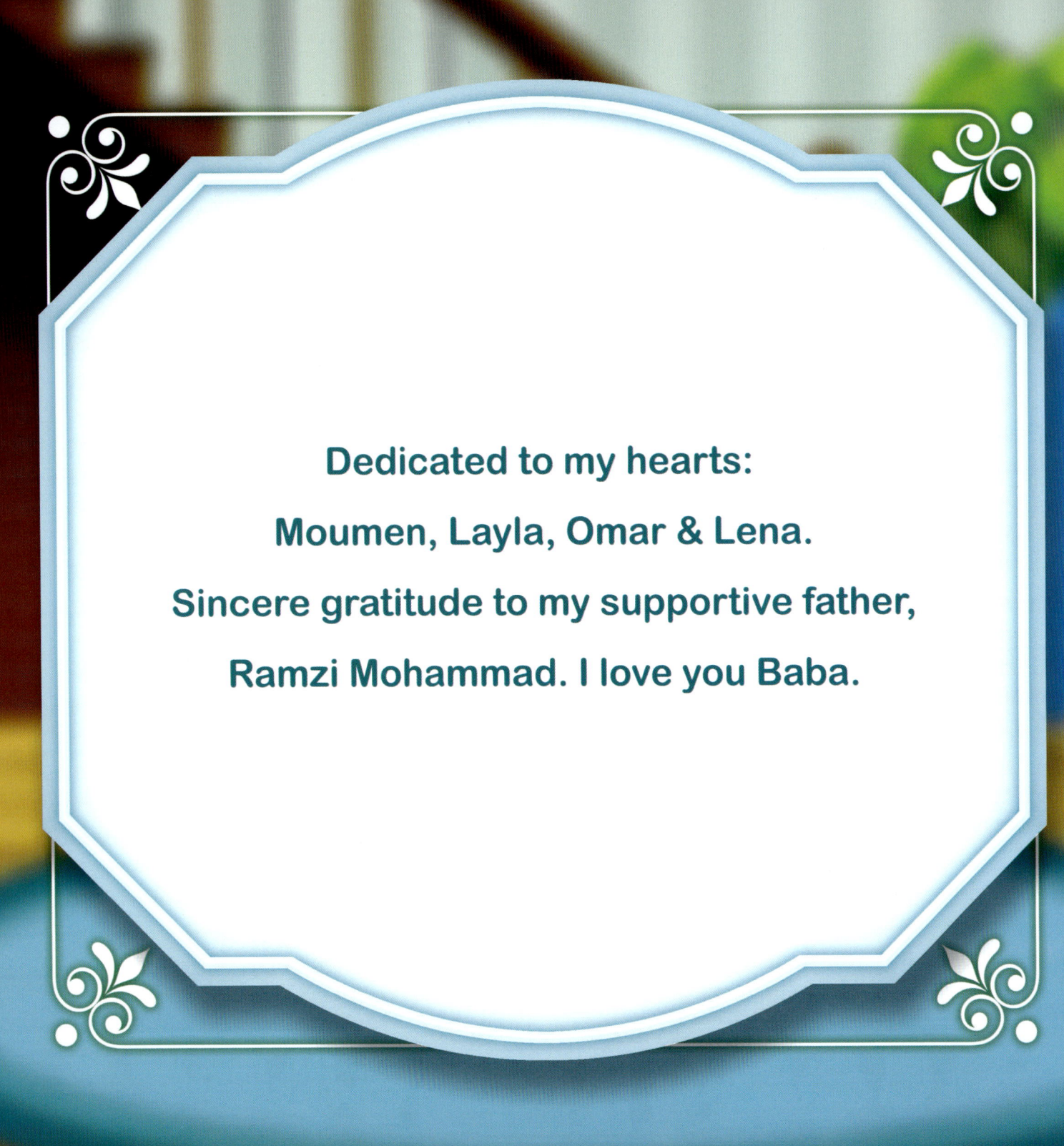

Dedicated to my hearts:

Moumen, Layla, Omar & Lena.

Sincere gratitude to my supportive father,

Ramzi Mohammad. I love you Baba.